Path towards Healing & Oneness

Self help

Calvina Braganza

 pencil

ISBN 978-93-5610-560-7
© Calvina Braganza 2022
Published in India 2022 by Pencil

A brand of
One Point Six Technologies Pvt. Ltd.
123, Building J2, Shram Seva Premises,
Wadala Truck Terminal, Wadala (E)
Mumbai 400037, Maharashtra, INDIA
E connect@thepencilapp.com
W www.thepencilapp.com

DISCLAIMER: *The opinions expressed in this book are those of the authors and do not purport to reflect the views of the Publisher.*

Author biography

Book written by
Calvina Braganza
Born A Spiritual being with emmense talents and gifts the
writer has powerful resources through personal experience

CONTENTS

Preface

Acknowledgements

This book is dedicated to my beloved soul sister Dolvyn and also my best friend Leontia whom I met on my way to healing and spiritual journey towards enlightenment

My experience with Spiritual Awakening Process

My experience it's spiritual awakening process loneliness depression OCD chronic anxiety last and long lasting for many years experience in The dark Knight of the soon when you witness The dark Knight of the soul is just a Peter period of auto spiritual disolation disconnection in emptiness which one feels totally separated from the divine those who experience it will feel totally lost hopeless and consume with melancholy it's a type of spiritual depression if a man wishes to sure on the road he is travelling on he must close his eyes and travel in the dark like being in the above got this emptiness the modern understanding of having a dark Knight of the soul is how ever is not exclusively just one but can offer mean losing all meaning in life feeling out of touch with the divine feeling bittrade of a second by life and having no solid or stable ground stand on some of the heavy questions we asked during the period why am I alive why do people suffer what is the truth is there god after life what is the point of living dark Knight of the soul is one the same as depression it can open be treated and sometimes cure with medication cognitive behaviour therapy mindfulness practices lifestyle changes and so on for the more depression has its roots in biological chemical imbalances and healthy thought patterns and open comes is result of personal loss mental illness physical illness substance abuse

Introduction

What I mean is self awareness this happens in soul searching attaining Oneness there is so much pain in the world and that is due to separation which is clinical terms known as fragmentation there are many reasons and the root cause is due to wounded inner-child rising on the pillar of shame, guilt and loneliness and due to emptiness and other negative emotions results in self hate. Due to resentment all the energy gets stagnated and all intuitive powers go on tapped resulting into energy blockages causing energy imbalance of the seven chakras in the human body. They were creating other issues in Mental Health physical emotional well being they were affecting our relationships when a child is born he or she is born with connectedness and Oneness. Cutting the umbilical cord separates it the child from the mother breast milk increases the bond between mother and child as the child growth up it's without any ego on a judgement later the ego develops in adulthood and the adult self develops a sense of self and its Self-worth.

Finding yourself

The level of self esteem tells on the level of he is over vibration stay The spiritual alignment karma place an important role in law of mirroring it teachers as various lessons to relationships test and various lessons to learn law of Attraction is all about positive thinking you think can you attract your thoughts terms into words in your words into actions from your character and that shaves your personality self realization is the key to understanding on self and to so searching many of us a weekend for various reasons in particular especially when we feel that we cannot take up the insults and burning of a on soul when there is pain and suffering is one awakens layers get it like that of a onion ring and water means a small part after attaining Oneness on the path towards enlightenment it a curse gradually in waves and true layers in cycles like wise growing into a own new skin it is known as spiritual alchemy of once self.

Self -Love

Self love is the best form of cognitive behaviour therapy and a shortcut part towards Enlightenment it is a very easy to love one self and there are many ways to do it one simple way is to create positive thoughts and repeat it loudly in front of the mirror the also known as need of iner-work and other form is to practice self care taking good care on self health and hygiene and the list cause on and cutting of from toxic people who do not nourish our Soul making a simple change in your diet and lifestyle, saying prayers, connecting with the higher self, practicing other various Art therapy are learning a new skill or a hobby , researching on various other Self-help content. Self love is a good way to heal a trauma that is caused in early childhood meditation and self hypnosis are the best and very useful tools for healing and manifesting a deepest eyes and abundance through visualising I have heard of women losing weight and people coming out of addictions

Spiritual Alchemy

Going through a spiritual alchemy is one of the most confusing lonely alienating but also supremely beautiful experience is in life put simply spiritual awakenings mark the beginning of your initiation on The spiritual path without experience in spiritual awakening the go through out like pursuming the emptiness of money Fame power and respect in an attempt to find happiness there is no way you can plan for them to your life and she is everything them is that the hidden give very deep within them is that they occur at the precise time that you need them the most spiritual awakenings other souls cribe of freedom listen to its call and your life will be transform into something meaningful and significant refuse is call and your life will be a graveyard if you have experience to spiritual awakening you have come to see through the lies and illusions of the world deep in your soul you realise that nothing external has ever and ever can ever bring you they happiness of fullfilment this profound realization lives you craving for something that will make you feel hole awareness again if you are looking for answers if you are thirsty for a direction in like this page will share with you everything you need to know you will find all the possible resources you need for the beginning of your journey including spiritual awakening symptoms and much more

What is Spiritual Awakening

Spiritual Ascensiontial is a wake up to life the begin to question all believes habits and social conditioning and see that there is much more to life then what we have been thought is common to ask questions why am I here what is the purpose of my life what happens after that why to good peoples of her and the questions that exam in the fundamental nature of life during your awakening spiritual awake names start the depressed and most significant questions with in us that we have been putting of asking to scared to touch if you are experienced a spiritual awakening you my crave to find the meaning of your life and weather there is a higher state of being searching of God of the divine is a common desired during this experience. It is a United present women force constantly evolving maturing healing and embroidering the divine that I am in separable a part of the benefit of writing down your thoughts is that you will be able to refer back to them in the future and see how your approach has more shared and evolved.

Five types of Spiritual Ascension

Also known as spiritual awakening is a natural evolutionary process which involves the process of shading the old self and experience many people speak about spiritual essential in terms of being upgraded rebooted or being in elevated in vibrational frequency all of these terms away from referring to the evolution and expansion of the mind heart in soul as the name employed the heart of soul as an is reaching you hurts and transcending old limiting the lips habits minds it's and ways of being spiritual essential is not chess inches unicorns and roses it is open accompany and shocking ships that result in what is known as the dark Knight of the soul

Awakening of the mind & welcoming Synchronicities

Awakening of the mind

Synchronisty of reveals the meaning of connection between the subjective and objective world you keep seeing the same repetitive numbers colors words for images all the time to it , repetitive numbers such as 11.11 4343 remaining about people animals places then seeing them repeatedly the tree of life is actor meeting the exact right person at the exact right time of the day

How to welcome into your life be mindful and away practice a lotus and be attention to the present moment

Be open and receptive maintain and open mind Outlook towards internship this will hence your receptors experienc

The humble sometimes what you desire or thing is the best for yourself and is not learn to have a very loose hold on your desires in this way you won't be imposing yourself you will allow life to impose itself on you be trusting your life and when it does trust individual and follow the path presented the head of you when you learn to trust your self ,also learn to trust life following the instinct listen to what you are got instead, is telling you your own just mind is was limitless and extreme open for all the time and when you choose to listen to an instance.

Authencity

Finding your soul within the dreams of reality. Why is it so hard to apply to your life and why is it so hard to be yourself? A person fails to listen to their inner souls and instead create a mental ideas and dreams of what they should be like and begin to doubt themselves whether they are living up to them afterward they see comforting validation by asking questions like is it what spiritual people do? if I can't do this does that mean I am not an empathic person? and do all healers and old souls, yogis are like this and that , in this article I want to explore a lost authencity and how we can learn to find a genuine cells by learning to love ourselves . A childs Authenticity is watching children play and hearing the general laughter is one of the greatest beauties in life for all born as children fill with life sense of Wonder and the desires to explore or create and leave in the moment children have no pass baggage of you sayings it so the Express for the feel and afraid to love on conditionerly after the age of 3 ever children start to become more tame this happens to all of us something changes within us and we begin to lose that wonder that's Innocence of childhood or thoughts become a modem in putting authentic feelings in the background slowly we begin to focus only on this thoughts and in doing so we came to accumulate past baggage and overcome future anxieties.

Sense of Self-worth

This process of losing your authencity and replacing it with the thoughts in the form of yours shameful memories rules social values and believes is known as domestication that can turn into a disease if our parents do not have the awareness and wisdom of what they are passing on towards just like pets we are domesticated with an emotional reward of punishment system if a behaviour ise are rewarded with a attention and affection if ouro behaviour we are punished by the rejection if a parents of tears as children we didn't care about peoples opinions or judgements will lived in the present in ourself worth came from our authencity now ever thoughts are more predominant with thoughts and suddenly I need to be accepted grows a self work is now put into the hands of the other people and their opinions of us this new cell was systeme is a change it forces to create false image of ourselves a dream slowly we begin to no to set different people expect different things from us ,parents our teachers our friends our bosses, siblings , lovers and so we are split into dozens of different versions of self ,we becomes so good at leaving after the different images of our selves that we forget really when , what determines from your false self image instead of your authentic you constantly feel of centre and shares and incomplete deep down your unconscious knows this image of yourself isn't true keep down you know that you are pretending the danger is if your falls image is that of being a smart person you are from to have yoursel is that you are having your self worth shattered publicly if someone outsmarts you. This is when we learn to hate ourselves.

Waking up your authentic self

Can you imagine the chaos that trying to find love and approval outside of ourselves create in the world except because we are so afraid of getting rejected but until we learn to love ourselves we will never be able to truly love anybody else. How do we stop being self destructive we have to stop pretending to be something we are not and find authencity again there are some practical suggestions that I have experienced myself and witness to work out quite well. Be honest with yourself to find your authencity again you are going to need one key ingredient with yourself you find what is real in yourself and what is the lie what you have either is inherited from your domestication beliefs values ambitions or unconsciously created as a defence mechanism to protect your false self image. This is your mind finding a label to try to live up to a false image Learn how to forgive yourself you can be a own worst enemy one of the first steps is finding your authentic self is to stop charging yourself and weather or not your leaving up to the first perfection standards and expectations you have said yourself the easiest way to overcome self judgement is to learn how to forgive yourself you repeat the same cycle over and over again creating soothing comfort becomes a wishes cycle unhealthy patterns are not good for you your mind. Self love and respect loving yourself is not selfish in fact it's the only way we can bring about any positive change we can never be happy unless we learn to love a cells on conditionally to love yourself is to have self respect to treat your body like the temple eating a healthy tired cleanliness and exercise as well as respecting your emotional and psychological help by avoiding the acculation of emotional poison gorgeous heated and impatience embrace being alone I can never stressed this enough making time for solitude by creating space for authensity it is solitude that we become aware of a domestication realising that what we are truly like in a own company when we are in putting on a false image for other people or tensity will teach you to see the wall as it is not as you believe it to be you are the manifestation of the divine within a body coming to your own soul as you become more than that you will understand this not with logic and your social personality but feeling it at the route of your core very existence

Inner work

Inner work is the psychological and special practice of diving deep into your inner self for the purpose of self exploration self understanding healing in spiritual transformation when we do in our shining the light of awareness on to inner landscape which is composed to the various layers of a mind ,the conscious, subconscious and conscious consist of your hidden feelings memories thoughts believes prejudice shadows another mental emotional conditions that influence your ability to transform and feel the whole at a core level by doing inner work you will be able to move limitations depression fears addictions and the feelings of wholeness that tend to plague us as human beings.

Three profound in a work pathways self love it's one of the most gentle and approachable in a work parts but that doesn't dilute or negative importance self love can land itself to been shallow necessary self indulgent but be the right training self love can go bone Deep and generally transform you at the cool level I always recommend self love is the best starting place without building a good relationship with yourself The other forms of inner work lifted below may be two intimidating and difficult of plane and old determine one of my favourite forms of self love is need a work s quite simply involves using a mirror to clearly see your insecurities and fears it also connect you with Deepa essence of yourself that is full of unconditional compassion forgiveness and exceptions of your soul in a child work one level deep is inner child work a form of inner work that involves examining your childhood bones here and believes to different degrees we All carry a wounded in a child story in a child work

Shadow work

At the deepest level of Innova process is Shadow work this form of inner work is the most complex allusive and intermediateing of all which Shadow work we are literally exploding the darkest places of a psyche that we are deliberately suppress then I and the zone each and every day we all know what looks in the shadows the spine chilling stuff of nightmares Shadow work is the process of practicing exploring your inner demons within your shadow locks everything that has been outlord deemed tab you bad ugly and unexpectable by your parents in society your shadow self contains all that you are secretly your shame about and disgustd by within yourself before attempting Shadow work it is absolutely imperative that you practice tell flower you must have stable and healthy self esteem before doing Shadow work in easily make you feel thousand times was about yourself you have poor self that is not for beginners if you had some experience with inner work I recommend approaching Shadow box slowly Oracle and tarot cards are a great way to begin with exploring your shadows as well as mindful journaling.

Practicing mindfulness

Everyday practicing mindfulness is best in the morning through active meditation sit in erect posture think of your body is a majestic mountain then settle into your breath notice the old sensation is it comes in your nostril and as it goes out of your mouth you can also focus of your body thought sensations memories and feelings will arise and pull you away at first but you must try yourself back towards the breath becoming aware of them for the first you weak so I won't this will be difficult task continue mindfulness practice each day make a judgements as you see it and experiment what works best for you. Notice external triggles see of weaknesses loss bad late night bad habits shopping too much excessive social media and other toxic habits closely exam in them notice uncomfortable feelings and sensations become a way of the feelings associated with your story this feelings about emotional and also sensory based for example body shift muscles clan shows hot beat rate become away of your figures and take a lot of practice without avoidance face all your fears without avoidance consciously allow yourself to feel the mental emotional and physical triggers that arise during your day notice your tendency to run away from them dramatized them or district or cell from them except this and show yourself compassion allow yourself to open up and to whatever you feel notice it temporally allow it to

pass in in an out of conjunis become your own best friend
ask yourself how would I treat myself in your story

25

Spiritual Oneness

Oneness can be felt by anyone there is no secret or elite club here no matter what agent is background intellectual level of spiritual development you have one is your destiny in other words not only you have the right to experience it but it is an integrated part of your journey of a spiritual seeker and ultimately another words it is wise the explanation of best ways to directly feel and embody this nature is the existence of your true nature or secret original state of being one is an experience the mind one feels a connection with everything in existence on every level in other words we feel at one with all things and other way to put is that feeling of fullness and completion it is experience of embedded nature the cell that exist beyond limited personalities other names for non dual awareness Buddha nature, Christ consciousness and enlightenment.

How to experience Oneness

There is no instant peel for experiencing Oneness and wholeness. I recommend to turn out some buzzfeed chickpet advise because that would this on a house really deep the path of ones is countless people have spend your entire lives on this path so with the atmos respect for the true commitment and sincerity mindfulness and meditation it goes hang in hand and a vento the mainstream market certainly to approach many modern teachers have towards meditation is secularised and water down but there are many ancient techniques such as the personal through awareness and breathing awareness meditation which helps you to gain direct inside to into the nature of your mind fulness is another simple mindfulness being attention to the present and more about the shopping of your awareness and ability to live in the present moment can we experience to this two popular practices.

Solitary nature immersion spelling time alone surrounded by nature is another beautiful way of accessing a state of holders and one nurse training and cell to simply observed nature as a passive form of meditation is narration to the soul and can fill you with the healing sense of inner peace I have found it myself so that by the presence of trees and birds around me that I have a temporally become one with everything around me nature emotion is a powerful practice for many mental and physical elements so it is worth with experimenting plant medicine in a work that focuses on integration there are many forms of inner work but not all of them focus on exploring accepting an integrating the repressed and rejected parts of you while this Park can be slow it is my perspective and experience the deepest work you can do that is no quick fix is here to have more than fleeting dreams of Oneness you must make the unconscious conscious you must seek to reunite to The Lost part of a cells and developed psychological balance only then can we experience of 10th experiment in a work include Shadow work and inner child work real self love compassion and acceptance love is the most expensive feeling and reality when we truly and generally love someone or something from the death of a beam all barriers are tone down strucks all division integrates all that remains openness expensiveness and yes the experience of humans having a spiritual experience we had a complex relationship with the cells that is often define by extreme highs and loss sometimes we think that the cats pajamas and other times feel like a file of toad but if we can manage to embrace to both high and Lowes and truly understands the nature of a mines we can experience real self love and hears how to love ourself smooth we can embrace both are humanity and experience self compassion self acceptance please call it is and practices essentials on The Spiritual path without learning to love a cells in all of your nurse and secred nurse is impossible to fully open to the experience of holness and.

Conclusion

I would conclude with all these practices that consistency is the key to building up with discipline and with practice and patience the results will be much fruitful and tremendous. I would recommend each person to follow all the methods and steps religiously.

My personal experience was so blissful and joyful. Not only did it empower me Spiritually but mentally, physically, emotionally and various other aspects in all the answers I was looking out for .

An answer to all my prayers.

www.ingramcontent.com/pod-product-compliance
Lightning Source LLC
La Vergne TN
LVHW040726170726
843469LV00079B/1295